Caring for Your
Chinchilla

Heather C. Hudak

Weigl Publishers Inc.

Project Coordinator
Heather C. Hudak

Design
Warren Clark

Published by Weigl Publishers Inc.
350 5th Avenue, Suite 3304, PMB 6G
New York, NY 10118-0069
Web site: www.weigl.com

Library of Congress Cataloging-in-Publication Data

Hudak, Heather C., 1975-
  Caring for your chinchilla / Heather C. Hudak.
    p. cm. -- (Caring for your pet)
  Includes index.
  ISBN 1-59036-466-X (lib. bdg. : alk. paper) -- ISBN 1-59036-467-8 (softcover : alk. paper)
  1. Chinchillas as pets--Juvenile literature. I. Title. II. Series: Caring for your pet (Mankato, Minn.)
  SF459.C48H83 2007
  636.935'93--dc22

                              2006016100

                    Printed in the United States of America
                    1 2 3 4 5 6 7 8 9 0   10 09 08 07 06

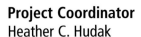

Locate the chinchilla paw prints throughout the book to find useful tips on caring for your pet.

Photograph and Text Credits
Every reasonable effort has been made to trace ownership and to obtain permission to reprint copyright material. The publishers would be pleased to have any errors or omissions brought to their attention so that they may be corrected in subsequent printings.

Rebecca Szulhan & Janelle Jeffrey: pages 15, 16, 21 top.

Cover: Chinchillas are friendly, energetic animals that make great pets.

Contents

CHINCHILLA NESTING BOX
CHIN NEST

Chilling with Chinchillas

Chinchillas are great pets. Their soft fur and small size make them a common pet in households across the world. Chinchillas are smart, clean, and friendly, and they do not need much space. Still, these cute animals require a great deal of special care. Chinchillas have fragile bones and cannot be held often. They also like to chew and **gnaw** furnishings.

Each chinchilla has her own personality. Some enjoy being held, while others prefer to walk on their own. Some chinchillas sleep all day, and others are very playful.

In nature, chinchillas live in rocky places. They spend much of their time hiding in cracks and crevices.

Having a pet chinchilla is a big responsibility. It is important to play with a pet chinchilla every day. Chinchillas also need fresh food and water daily. Owners must be sure to provide what their pet needs to live a happy and healthy life. If you give your chinchilla plenty of love and attention, she will return your affection.

■■■ Chinchillas love to chew. Pet chinchillas will chew on anything they find inside their cage.

Fascinating Facts

- Chinchillas belong to the rodent group. Rodents are small, nibbling animals. They have four teeth called incisors that grow continually. Hamsters, guinea pigs, gerbils, mice, porcupines, and rats are other rodents.
- Chinchillas do not sweat. This means that if the weather is hot, their body becomes very warm. If they cannot cool off, they might die.

Pet Profiles

In nature, there are three chinchilla **species**. These are *brevicaudata*, *lanigera*, and *costina*. Brevicaudata are short-tailed chinchillas that have a flat, square face with a thick neck. Lanigera are long-tailed. They have a narrow head and shoulders, and long ears. Costina chinchillas look like mice or rats. They have a narrow face with long, thin ears and a lengthy tail.

BLACK VELVET

- Also known as "touch of velvet"
- Has dark fur on its head, back, and sides
- Has a white belly
- First appeared in 1960

SAPPHIRE

- Has a light gray body with a blue shine
- Has a white belly
- Has black eyes and dark ears
- First bred in Indiana in the 1960s

PINK WHITE

- Has a white body with beige patches
- Has red eyes and pink ears
- Nose is bright pink
- Paws and belly are white

Chinchillas found in nature are a light gray color. Since they were first brought to North America in the early 1900s, however, several new color variations have occurred. Chinchilla colors now range from white to violet, but the most common color is gray. The color of the animal does not affect his personality or health.

EBONY

- Has dark, silky, glossy fur all over its body
- Has black eyes and dark ears
- Very calm; good-natured
- First appeared in the 1960s

VIOLET

- Has violet or steely gray fur and a white belly
- Has black eyes with dark ears
- First appeared in Rhodesia, South Africa, in 1960
- First shown in the United States in 1967

STANDARD

- Has gray fur that is darkest on the back and lighter on the sides
- Has a white belly
- Has black eyes and gray or black ears
- Paws have a dark stripe

Changing Chinchillas

Chinchillas first lived in the Andes Mountains of Peru, Chile, and Bolivia. **Indigenous peoples** in these areas made clothing and other items from chinchillas' rich, soft fur. When European explorers first visited South America in the 1500s, they were impressed with the chinchilla furs they saw. The explorers returned to Europe with a few **pelts**, which they gave as gifts to very important people. Clothing made from chinchilla fur quickly became very popular in Europe.

■ In the Andes, chinchillas can be found living in places more than 2,600 feet (800 meters) high.

Europeans began trapping thousands of wild chinchillas to make clothing. During the 1800s, more than one million chinchillas were trapped. Too much hunting greatly decreased the number of chinchillas in nature. In the early 1900s, laws were passed to stop people from hunting so many of these animals.

Chinchillas were first brought to North America in the 1920s. A man named Mathias F. Chapman trapped 11 chinchillas in Chile. He brought them home to the United States and began **breeding** them. Chapman raised some of the animals for their fur. Others, he sold as pets. Today, most pet chinchillas in North America are descended from "Chapman chinchillas."

Baby chinchillas should be petted often so they will be friendly as adults.

▬ Today, few chinchillas live in nature.

Fascinating Facts

- The word *chinchilla* means "Little Chincha." The animals were named after the Chincha peoples of the Andes Mountains. These indigenous peoples wore chinchilla furs.
- Chinchillas are descended from animals called Megamys that lived more than 250 million years ago.
- Only three of the chinchillas Chapman trapped were female.

Life Cycle

In nature, chinchillas live about 10 years. Pet chinchillas live twice as long, to about 20 years of age. With proper care, they can live even longer. A chinchilla has different needs at each stage of his life. At all life stages, a pet chinchilla will depend on his owner for love and attention.

Newborn Chinchillas

Newborn chinchillas are called kits. Unlike newborn hamsters or rabbits, kits are covered with fur. They look like smaller versions of their parents. Kits open their eyes soon after they are born. They weigh about 1.2 ounces (35 grams). Kits can eat solid food when they are 1 week old.

Mature Chinchillas

Chinchillas mature at different times. As chinchillas become older, their coats may begin to dull. They may lose their fur, too. Mature chinchillas will sleep more and play less. They are also more likely to become ill.

Fascinating Facts

- It is difficult to tell if a female chinchilla is pregnant. A veterinarian can feel her stomach carefully for babies. Weighing the chinchilla often is another way to tell if she is pregnant.
- Female chinchillas may begin to sleep on their side or in strange positions if they are pregnant.

Six to Eight Weeks

When kits are 6 to 8 weeks of age, they stop drinking their mother's milk. They must stay with their mother until they are at least 8 weeks of age. Young chinchillas can have babies. However, they are too young to be good parents. For this reason, males and females should be kept apart.

Adult Chinchillas

At about 8 months of age, chinchillas are adults. They are ready to have babies. A mother chinchilla will carry her babies in her belly for about 111 days. She will give birth to two or three babies in each litter. Adult chinchillas grow to about 10 inches (25 centimeters) long and weigh 1 to 2 pounds (500 to 800 grams).

Picking Your Pet

Choosing a chinchilla is a big responsibility. There are many things to consider before selecting a new pet. The following questions will help you decide if a pet chinchilla is right for you.

Chinchillas are nocturnal. This means they sleep during the day and are active at night.

Where Can I Buy a Chinchilla?

▬ Many pet owners find that chinchillas are entertaining pets with plenty of personality.

Chinchillas are available at many pet stores. These animals make great pets for first-time buyers. However, if you are looking for a specific species or color of chinchilla, you may need to go to a **breeder**. Breeders have more animals to choose from than pet stores. Chinchilla breeders also know a great deal about the animals they raise. They can provide information and tips about how to care for your new pet. Often, chinchillas raised by breeders have had plenty of human contact and will be more comfortable around their new owners. Sometimes, it also is possible to adopt a chinchilla from an animal shelter, such as the local Society for the Prevention of Cruelty to Animals (SPCA).

Can Chinchillas Be Trained?

Chinchillas are very smart animals. Some chinchillas recognize their names when they are called. Others can be taught to do tricks, such as "sit up." Each time your chinchilla performs a trick, reward her with affection and treats. Over time, she will learn to do the trick on command.

■■■ Although chinchillas are nocturnal, many can be trained to wake up for playtime during the day.

What Should I Look for When Picking my Chinchilla?

Try to choose a chinchilla that is in good health. Visit the breeder or pet store at night, when chinchillas are most active. A healthy chinchilla should be plump and lively. She should have clean, bright eyes, and the fur under her chin should be dry. She should not be missing patches of fur, and her coat should be shiny. Be sure that your chinchilla is at least 10 weeks old before you bring her home.

Fascinating Facts

- Chinchillas need time to get to know their owners. This may take days, weeks, or even months. Once your chinchilla is comfortable with you, she will show a great deal of affection. She may rub her head against your hand and softly **chuckle**. This means that she is happy.

Chinchilla Chests

Moving to a new home can be stressful for any animal. To help make your chinchilla feel comfortable, you should be prepared with some basic equipment. The most important equipment you will need is a cage. Chinchillas need a wire cage that is at least 2 feet long by 2 feet wide (0.6 meters long by 0.6 m wide). Some cages have two levels. This provides pet chinchillas with plenty of room to run and play. If the cage has only one level, it is a good idea to add a shelf or a perch where your chinchilla can sit.

Cedar and redwood shavings are poisonous to chinchillas.

When picking a cage, be sure it has a solid tray bottom. Chinchillas' feet can become caught in wire cage bottoms. They may chew off their own foot or break a leg if they fall between the wires. Line the tray with white pine shavings, since colored shavings may stain the chinchilla's fur. Be sure to change the shavings at least once a week.

■ Chinchillas should be kept in metal cages. They can chew their way out of plastic or wood shelters.

A pet chinchilla will need a water bottle mounted on the side of his cage. The water bottle will release liquid slowly while the chinchilla licks the tip. Do not put a water bowl inside your chinchilla's cage. If his fur becomes wet, it may be ruined. However, you should put a food bowl inside the cage, and be sure to provide your pet with a piece of wood for gnawing.

■ Chinchillas do not overeat. They only eat as much as they need to feel full.

Fascinating Facts

- Chinchillas are happiest and healthiest in rooms that have a temperature between 60° and 70° Fahrenheit (16° and 21° Celsius). If the room is too warm, chinchillas can become ill.
- Like cats, ferrets, and some guinea pigs, chinchillas can be trained to use a litter box.

Chinchilla Chips

Chinchillas are herbivores, which means they only eat plant matter. They do not eat any meat. Pet chinchillas should be fed twice a day: once in the morning and again at night. Chinchillas should eat good quality food pellets. Pellets have special **nutrients** that chinchillas need to stay healthy. A chinchilla eats about 2.2 pounds (1 kilogram) of pellets each month or about 2 tablespoons (30 milliliters) per day. Chinchillas should also eat plenty of hay and alfalfa.

Be sure to provide your chinchilla with fresh water each day.

■ Dried banana chips can make a tasty treat for pet chinchillas.

Fascinating Facts

- Chinchillas like to have a routine. They will look for food at the same time each day.
- Chinchillas can chew on a cuttlefish bone. This provides calcium and helps wear down their teeth.

Chinchillas should not be fed food mixtures. Mixes often include treats. Your chinchilla will only eat the items she likes, which will not provide a balanced diet.

Chinchillas can have treats such as raisins, pumpkins seeds, shredded wheat, and nuts. Only give your pet one treat each day. If a chinchilla eats too many treats, she may become fat and unhealthy. Never feed your pet cabbage, lettuce, or corn. These foods can cause stomach problems that may cause a chinchilla to become ill.

■ A single raisin or nut is a good treat for a chinchilla. Some chinchillas may also enjoy small pieces of kiwi fruit as a special snack.

From Feet to Fur

Although there are many different colors of chinchillas, most have the same features. All chinchillas grow to be about the same size and weight. They all have a plump, round body, soft, thick fur, large ears, bushy tails, and fragile bones.

▬ **Chinchilla**

A chinchilla's teeth never stop growing. They can grow up to 12 inches (30 cm) each year.

Chinchilla fur is very soft. It is also odorless. Chinchillas do not have **dander**. Their fur does not carry pests, such as fleas. Fleas cannot breathe in a chinchilla's thick fur.

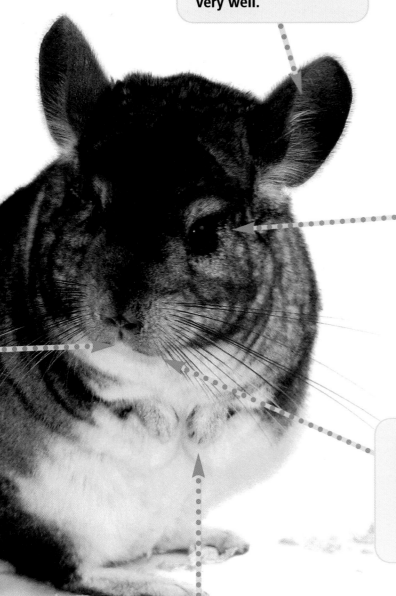

Chinchillas have long ears that are nearly hairless. They can hear very well.

Chinchillas do not see well. They memorize objects in their environment to avoid running into them. Chinchillas have night vision, so they see as well at night as they do during the day. Some chinchillas have red eyes, making them very **sensitive** to light.

Like humans, chinchillas use sounds to communicate with each other and their owners. They can make many different sounds. Happy chinchillas might make a soft grunting sound.

Chinchillas have short front legs that end in small **forepaws**. Their paws have four fingers and a thumb, which they use to hold their food. Chinchillas also have long hind legs that allow them to move forward quickly by jumping or hopping.

Keeping Clean

Chinchillas are very clean animals. They are happiest when their home is neat and tidy. To keep your pet happy and healthy, clean his cage often. Remove soiled shavings and droppings, and wash feeding equipment such as bowls and water bottles. Remember to put fresh shavings, food, and water in the cage before letting your chinchilla back inside.

Like cats and dogs, chinchillas need to be groomed. Brushing your pet will remove loose fur and prevent **hairballs**. Chinchillas have sensitive skin and soft fur coats. Use a wire brush with small bristles to brush your pet's fur. The bristles on these brushes are not stiff and will not harm the animal. If your chinchilla does not like being brushed, roll a lint brush over her coat to remove dead fur.

In nature, chinchillas live in herds, or groups, of about 20 to 30 animals.

■ Chinchillas enjoy being groomed. When kept in pairs, they will spend much of their time grooming each other.

Chinchillas' fur should not become wet. Do not try to bathe your pet with water. Instead, your chinchilla can have a daily dust bath. Provide him with a special crushed **lava rock** in a dust bath box. Rolling in the dust for about 15 minutes will keep your chinchilla's fur from becoming **matted**.

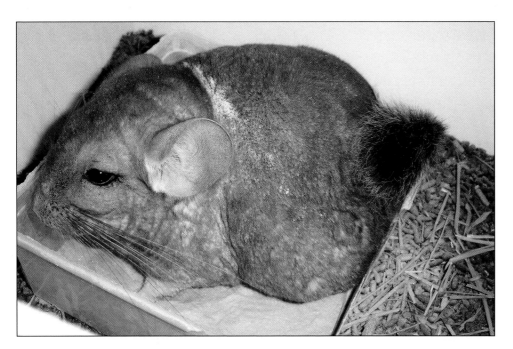

▬▬ Chinchillas need between 0.125 and 0.25 cups (30 and 60 ml) of dust to bathe.

Fascinating Facts

• Chinchillas file their teeth by gnawing on wood or **pumice stones**. Always be sure to have one of these items inside your pet's cage. If you use a wood block, be sure to change it often. The block can grow **fungus**, causing your chinchilla to become ill.

Healthy and Happy

Chinchillas should live in a cool, dry place. It is very important that they never become too hot. Pet chinchillas are most comfortable in temperatures that are cooler than 70°F (21°C). Take care to ensure there are no drafts blowing on your chinchilla or into her cage.

Chinchillas like to have a safe place to hide inside of their cage. A small house is the perfect place for a chinchilla to curl up on her back or side.

Chinchillas are very good at mazes. They memorize their trail, so they can find their way out quickly.

CHINCHILLA NESTING BOX
CHIN NEST

■ Chinchillas that share a cage should each have their own hiding space.

Chinchillas need plenty of exercise. To help, you can let your chinchilla run around a secure room. Be sure to remove any items that you do not want the chinchilla to gnaw. There are many toys available at pet stores that will also help your pet stay in shape. For example, it is a good idea to put a solid steel wheel inside your chinchilla's cage. Chinchillas enjoy running inside these wheels. Wire wheels are not safe, as your pet's leg can become caught in the spokes. Also make sure the wheel is large enough for your pet to fit comfortably inside without straining his back.

■ Chinchillas should be supervised when they play outside of their cage.

Fascinating Facts

- Chinchillas have thicker fur than any other land animal. They have 3,100 hairs per square inch (20,000 per square centimeter) of skin. Humans grow one hair per **follicle**. Chinchillas grow 80 per follicle.
- Most chinchillas will bite off their nails to keep them from growing too long. You can also use sandpaper to gently file down their nails.

Cheery Chinchillas

Before you bring home a pet chinchilla, you should have a cage, toys, and food supplies ready. It will take some time for your pet to feel comfortable in his new home. At first, the chinchilla may be quite shy. Be careful not to chase or frighten him. Place your hand inside his cage for your chinchilla to smell and touch. Soon, you will be able to touch your pet. Once your chinchilla is comfortable with you, he may rub his head against your hand. This means he wants to be scratched and petted.

It is not a good idea to travel with chinchillas. They do not like change.

■ Chinchillas will have a different relationship with every person they meet. Your chinchilla may act differently around you than with his breeder.

Pet Peeves

Chinchillas do not like:
- loud noises
- being held
- too much attention
- too little attention
- being too hot or too cold
- cedar shavings
- changing their routines

Chinchillas do not like being held. If you must handle your pet, place one hand under your chinchilla's shoulders, and use the other hand to support his rear legs. Hold the chinchilla firmly near your chest. Try picking up your pet a few times each day. Be sure to pet the animal lightly. Over time, your chinchilla will feel safe when you hold and pet him.

■ Chinchillas have varying personalities and moods.

Fascinating Facts

- More than one chinchilla can live in a single cage. Introduce chinchillas to one another slowly. Begin by keeping them in separate cages that are placed near each other. Let them get to know each other by visiting together in one cage for short periods. They may nibble or sniff each other, but over time, they likely will be able to live, cuddle, and play together.

Checking Chinchillas

After laws were passed to stop the hunting of wild chinchillas, people began breeding these animals on ranches. The first chinchilla ranch opened in South America in 1874. In the United States, the first ranches opened in the 1920s. Following World War II, the National Chinchilla Breeders of America, Inc. (NCBA) and the Farmers Chinchilla Cooperative of America (FCCA) were formed to help sell chinchilla furs. The two groups joined together to become Empress Chinchilla, which still sells furs today. Today, there are hundreds of chinchilla ranchers around the world.

Playful or frightened chinchillas might bite. If a chinchilla bites, gently blow in her face. Soon, she will learn that she should not bite.

Fascinating Facts

- At one time, the indigenous peoples of Chile thought chinchillas did not need to drink water or other liquids. Later, they learned that the animals got the water they needed by eating cactus parts.
- People have been keeping chinchillas as pets since the 1960s.

Today, many chinchilla owners enter their pets in shows. Chinchilla shows are held all over the world between May and October, when the weather is coolest. Prizes are awarded for the best chinchilla. Judges follow many rules and guides to decide which chinchilla has the **densest** fur, the best coloring, and is an ideal size and weight. Owners also receive awards for caring for their pets.

Chinchilla shows can be a great place to meet other pet owners as well as champion breeders.

Chinchilla Tales

In *Chinchilla Up the Chimney*, a chinchilla hides in Jean Knox's shopping bags. Before she can catch the animal, the chinchilla scurries away quickly. The chinchilla runs all around the house and even up the chimney. Jean tries everything she can think of to make the chinchilla come out of the chimney, but he will not budge. What will she do?

From Lucy Daniels' *Chinchilla Up the Chimney*.

Pet Puzzlers

How much do you know about chinchillas? If you can answer the following questions correctly, you may be ready to own a pet chinchilla.

Q How long do pet chinchillas live?

Pet chinchillas live for about 20 years.

Q Why do chinchillas need a piece of wood or a pumice stone in their cage?

Chinchillas need to chew on a piece of wood or a pumice stone to wear down their teeth.

Q What should a chinchilla be fed?

Chinchillas should be fed special pellets, hay, and alfalfa. They can also have treats, such as nuts, raisins, and shredded wheat.

Q Do chinchillas need to be bathed?

Chinchillas should take a daily dust bath in crushed lava rock.

Q What is special about chinchilla fur?

Chinchillas have very soft fur. They have about 80 hairs per follicle.

Q What color are chinchillas in nature?

In nature, chinchillas are a light gray color.

Q Where did chinchillas first come from?

The first chinchillas came from the Andes Mountains in South America.

Calling Your Chinchilla

Before you buy your pet chinchilla, write down some chinchilla names that you like. Some names may work better for a female chinchilla. Others may suit a male chinchilla. Here are just a few suggestions:

Max

Cherry

Chase

Grayson

Charlie

Chico

Poppy

Holly

Dusty

Frequently Asked Questions

Do chinchillas live well with other kinds of animals?

Chinchillas can get along well with rabbits and guinea pigs, but they should always be separated at mealtime and bedtime. Unlike most other animals, chinchillas have a special diet and must stay on a routine. Dogs, cats, and ferrets may try to attack your chinchilla, since they are natural enemies. It is not a good idea to leave chinchillas unsupervised around other kinds of animals.

Should I breed my chinchilla?

Breeding chinchillas is a very big responsibility. You should think carefully before putting a male and female together. A female chinchilla can have up to six babies at one time. The mother will care for the babies for only a few weeks after they are born. After that, it is your responsibility to care for the kits. You will need a larger cage and special food for the mother and babies.

Can my chinchilla chew on cardboard?

Chinchillas can chew on cardboard, as long as it is not printed with ink. Any cardboard you give your pet should be clean and dry. Bacteria may grow on wet cardboard. Chinchillas that chew on cardboard still need a wood block or pumice stone. Cardboard will not wear down their teeth, but it will give them something to tear apart. Make sure that your chinchilla does not each too much cardboard, since it can be unhealthy.

More Information

Animal Organizations

You can help chinchillas stay happy and healthy by learning more about them. Many organizations are dedicated to teaching people how to care for and protect their pet pals. For more chinchilla information, write to the following organizations.

Chinchillas.com
1265 160th Rd
Seneca, Kansas 66538

ChinWorld
24559 Via Las Laderas
Murrieta, CA 92562

Websites

To answer more of your chinchilla questions, go online and surf to the following websites:

Chinchilla World Industry Council
www.chinchillaindustrycouncil.com

Empress Chinchilla Breeders Cooperative, Inc.
www.harborside.com/~empressc

Chinchillarescue.org
www.chinchillarescue.org

Words to Know

breeder: someone who raises animals and sells them as pets

breeding: mating and raising animals

chuckle: to laugh softly or quietly

dander: flaky scales of skin or fur

densest: having parts that are very close together

follicle: the small opening that is around the root of a hair

forepaws: front paws

fungus: a plant-like organism that appears as a fuzz on the skin

gnaw: wear away by nonstop biting or chewing

hairballs: clumps of hair inside an animal's stomach

indigenous peoples: original inhabitants of the land

lava rock: made when the hot, melted rock from a volcano cools and hardens

matted: a tangled clump of knots

mazes: connecting passages through which it is easy to become lost

nutrients: the nourishing parts of foods

pelts: animal skins

pumice stones: grayish rocks that are used to smooth or polish

sensitive: to feel things strongly

species: a group of related animals

Index